W9-BFV-918

Mesopotamia

SUNITA APTE

Children's Press®
An Imprint of Scholastic Inc.
New York Toronto London Auckland Sydney
Mexico City New Delhi Hong Kong
Danbury, Connecticut

Content Consultant
Karen L. Wilson
Kish Project Coordinator, Field Museum
Research Associate, Oriental Institute, University of Chicago

Library of Congress Cataloging-in-Publication Data

Apte, Sunita.
  Mesopotamia / by Sunita Apte.
      p. cm.—(A true book)
  Includes index.
   ISBN-13: 978-0-531-25230-7 (lib. bdg.)   978-0-531-24111-0 (pbk.)
   ISBN-10: 0-531-25230-2 (lib. bdg.)   0-531-24111-4 (pbk.)

1. Iraq—History—To 634—Juvenile literature. I. Title. II. Series.

DS71.A627 2009
935—dc22   2008054304

1 2 3 4 5 6 7 8 9 10 R 19 18 17 16 15 14 13 12 11   62

Find the Truth!

Everything you are about to read is true *except* for one of the sentences on this page.

Which one is **TRUE**?

T or F The ancient Mesopotamians were the first to use the wheel.

T or F Persia was once part of ancient Mesopotamia.

Find the answers in this book.

Assyrian wall carving

Ishtar Gate

Contents

THE BIG TRUTH!

An Ancient World Wonder

Mesopotamian cities were built along the Euphrates River.

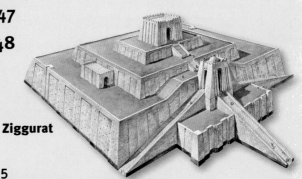

Ziggurat

The town of Erbil (EAR-bill) is in northeastern Iraq. It is believed to be one of the oldest cities that still exists from Mesopotamia.

CHAPTER 1

An Ancient Land

More than 5,000 years ago, the world's first large towns and cities were built in a region called Mesopotamia (mezz-oh-poh-TAY-mee-uh). Mesopotamia was located in what is now the country of Iraq. The Mesopotamians were actually many different groups of people that lived in this area over thousands of years. These groups of people made up some of the world's first **civilizations** (si-ve-li-ZAY-shens).

 Mesopotamia is sometimes called the "cradle of civilization."

Land of Beginnings

In addition to being the first place where cities sprang up, Mesopotamia was also one of the places where people first mastered farming. Because so many important things first happened in Mesopotamia, it has been called "the cradle of civilization."

In fact, many of the things in your life were first used in Mesopotamia. Experts believe that Mesopotamians were the first people to use a written language. **Archaeologists** (ar-kee-OL-uh-jists) have also discovered that the use of the wheel, board games, and laws first took place in this region.

The "Royal Game of Ur" is the oldest board game ever found in the world.

Scientists found this game board and playing pieces in the remains of a cemetery in the Mesopotamian city-state of Ur (oor). It has been called the Royal Game of Ur. This discovery tells us that Mesopotamians were some of the first people to play a game like checkers or backgammon.

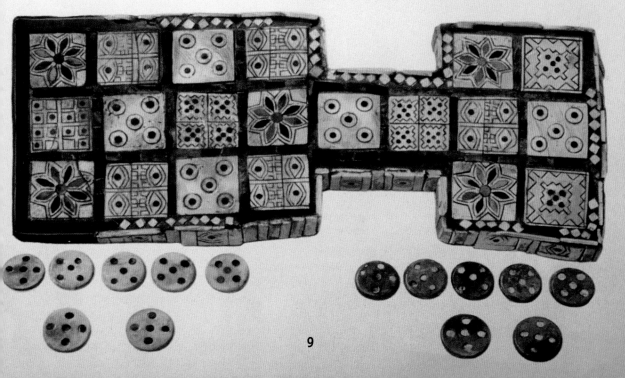

The town of Duhok is on the Tigris River in northern Iraq.

CHAPTER 2

Between the Rivers

Ancient Mesopotamia was part of the Fertile Crescent (FUR-tuhl KRESS-uhnt). The Fertile Crescent included all of the land north of the Persian Gulf, near the Tigris (TYE-gris) and Euphrates (yoo-FRAY-teez) Rivers, parts of Egypt, and what are today the countries of Israel, Syria, Jordan, Lebanon, and Iraq.

The word Mesopotamia means "the land between the rivers."

Farming Along the Rivers

Much of the land in the Fertile Crescent didn't get enough rain for growing crops. This made the Tigris and Euphrates important sources of water in ancient times. To get the river water to dry farmland, early settlers built canals. Each year, the two rivers would flood their banks. After the floods, a fine mud called **silt** would be left behind on the farmland. The silt helped crops grow better in the farmland of the Fertile Crescent.

Early settlers used wooden plows to soften the land for planting crops. They grew a wide variety of crops including wheat, onions, and dates. With so many crops, early settlers had plenty of food.

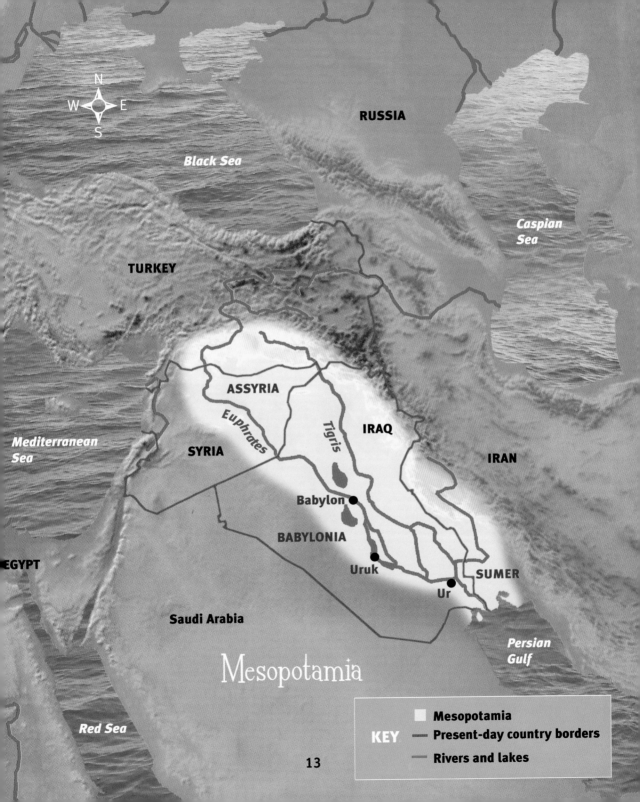

N
W   E
S

RUSSIA

Black Sea

Caspian Sea

TURKEY

ASSYRIA

Euphrates

Tigris

IRAQ

Mediterranean Sea

SYRIA

IRAN

Babylon ●

BABYLONIA

EGYPT

Uruk ●

SUMER

Ur ●

Saudi Arabia

Persian Gulf

Mesopotamia

Red Sea

13

KEY
  ■ **Mesopotamia**
  — **Present-day country borders**
  — **Rivers and lakes**

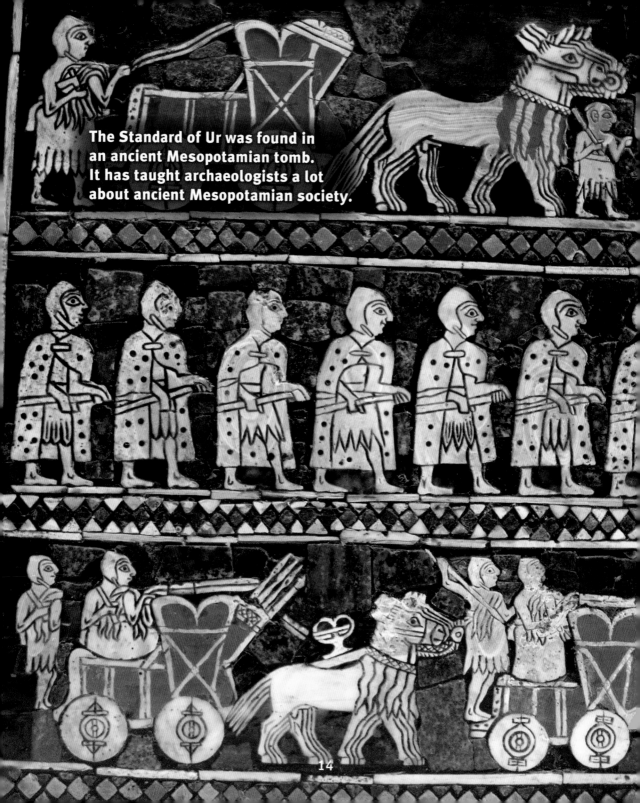

The Standard of Ur was found in an ancient Mesopotamian tomb. It has taught archaeologists a lot about ancient Mesopotamian society.

CHAPTER 3

City-States and Empires

Ancient Mesopotamia was not always one country. Instead, many different groups of people lived in this region. They often fought against each other in wars. Four of these groups are well-known for their accomplishments. They were the Sumerians (soo-MER-ee-uhns), the Akkadians (ah-KAD-ee-ans), the Babylonians (BAB-uh-loh-nee-uhns), and the Assyrians (uh-SEAR-ee-uhns).

Standard of Ur

Sumer

Experts believe Sumer (SOO-mur) was the world's first civilization. It began around 3500 B.C.E. in southern Mesopotamia. Instead of one government, Sumer was made up of about a dozen **city-states**. Every city-state had its own separate government, and each ruler wanted to make his city-state great. Uruk (YOO-ruk) was one of Sumer's first major cities. Experts believe it was the biggest city in the world at the time.

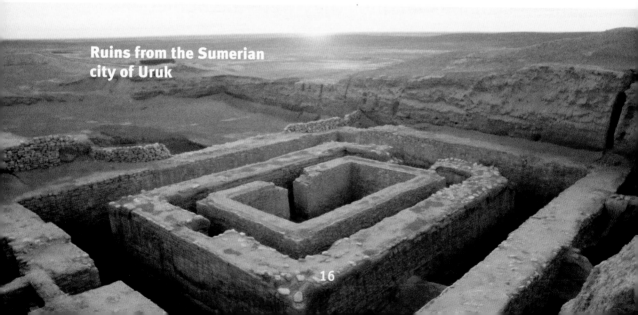

Ruins from the Sumerian city of Uruk

Sculpture of Sargon

The city-states of Sumer governed the region for hundreds of years. But in about 2300 B.C.E., Sargon, a king from Akkad (AK-kad) in northern Mesopotamia, took over Sumer. He created the world's first **empire** by bringing together southern and northern Mesopotamia under one ruler. But the Akkadians only ruled Sumer for 200 years before losing power. After this time, the empire broke up again into smaller kingdoms and city-states.

The First Wheel

Many archaeologists believe that the ancient Mesopotamians were the first to use the wheel. While no one is certain about when the wheel was invented, the earliest known one was found at the site of Kish, a Sumerian city-state that existed more than 5,000 years ago. The wheel is one of the world's most important inventions. It changed daily life for ancient people and made it easier to travel, farm, and shape clay into pottery.

The Assyrian Empire

The Assyrian Empire began in northern Mesopotamia more than 3,000 years ago in about 1100 B.C.E. The Assyrians were fierce warriors and conquered much of the Fertile Crescent over time. They were also great artists who created detailed sculptures and wall carvings. Typically, Assyrian art showed battle scenes and images of rulers with gods.

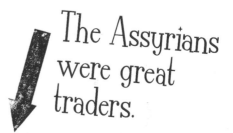

The Assyrians were great traders.

This stone carving shows Assyrian traders.

19

The Babylonian Empire

The Babylonian Empire was located in southern Mesopotamia and had two periods of greatness. The first began around 1790 B.C.E. when a king named Hammurabi (hah-mur-AH-bee) ruled. Under Hammurabi all of the separate cities were again united into one empire.

The capital city of Babylon (BAB-uh-lon) became the center of the entire Fertile Crescent. The Babylonians traded with faraway places. They were skilled sky watchers and mathematicians. The Babylonians also wrote long stories about their city and its history.

Mesopotamia Timeline

4000 B.C.E.
The city of Uruk is built.

2100 B.C.E.
Sumerian civilization reaches its height.

Hammurabi created a set of laws called the Code of Hammurabi. The code included 282 laws and the punishments for breaking them.

Eventually, the first Babylonian empire declined, or fell. But a thousand years later, a second Babylonian empire called New Babylonia began. New Babylonia's greatest emperor was Nebuchadnezzar (ne-be-ked-NE-zer) II, who rebuilt the city of Babylon. The walls and gates of the rebuilt city were so famous that even the ancient Greeks wrote about them.

1200 B.C.E.
The Assyrian Empire becomes more powerful.

625–539 B.C.E.
New Babylonia rules Mesopotamia.

21

Tall Tale or Truth?

Experts aren't sure if the Hanging Gardens of Babylon really existed. The ancient Greeks who first wrote about the gardens never actually saw them. And nothing was written about the gardens by the Babylonians themselves.

An Ancient World Wonder

The Hanging Gardens of Babylon were built by Nebuchadnezzar II for his wife, Amytis (AH-mih-tuhss). Amytis wasn't from Babylon, and missed the mountains and green plants of her homeland, Media, which is now part of Iran. So Nebuchadnezzar II built her a spectacular garden on the flat plains of Mesopotamia.

Beauty in Bloom

The Hanging Gardens of Babylon were made of terraces, or balconies that were filled with exotic plants and trees.

This bronze statue of Sumerian King Ur-Nammu (NAH-moo) was made in Mesopotamia in about 3000 B.C.E.

CHAPTER 4

Life in Mesopotamia

Archaeologists have learned about life in ancient Mesopotamia by studying **artifacts**, including pottery, artwork, and writing found on clay or stone tablets. Today, archaeologists are still searching the ruins of ancient cities and trying to find artifacts from different Mesopotamian civilizations.

King Ur-Nammu wrote the first known code of laws.

Homes

The remains of ancient cities show that the Mesopotamians built homes from bricks made of mud. Most homes had dirt floors and the outside walls were shared, like attached apartment houses today. There were outdoor courtyards where people may have had gardens and raised animals. Mesopotamian houses also had flat roofs. On warm nights, people may have slept on their rooftops.

An Iraqi soldier holds an ancient Mesopotamian artifact. Many valuable artifacts were stolen from the Iraq National Museum in Baghdad in 2003. Iraqi soldiers have recovered some of them.

Sumerian skirts were made of either animal skins or wool.

These three statues show men praying.

Clothing

Most of the information about Mesopotamian clothing comes from art such as sculptures and paintings. By studying artwork, archaeologists know that Sumerian men wore skirts and women wore shawls wrapped around their bodies. Not much is known about the Babylonians but it's believed that the men wore skirts and shawls. Assyrian men and women wore shawls over their entire bodies. Belts kept the shawls in place.

Gods and Religion

The Mesopotamians worshipped many gods. Each city-state had one main god that was its protector. Nanna (NAH-nah), the moon god, watched over the city of Ur. The main god of Babylon was Marduk (MAHR-dook), the supreme ruler over the entire universe. The Assyrians worshipped many of the same gods as the Sumerians and Babylonians.

Ruins of the city of Ur

28

Ziggurats were built on top of mud-brick platforms.

Many city-states built tall platforms with lots of steps called **ziggurats** (ZIH-gur-ats). About 25 still exist today. Ziggurats often had temples at the top. Experts believe that the temples were built for the gods of each city-state. It is thought that through the ziggurats, the Mesopotamians could be closer to their gods who lived in the sky. The only people allowed inside the temples may have been priests whose job it was to care for the gods.

Government

Ancient Mesopotamia had many rulers. For example, each Sumerian city-state had its own king. The Assyrian and Babylonian empires had rulers who were believed to have been chosen by the gods. They led the armies and acted as priests in the temples.

Mesopotamians kept records of their rulers on tablets called king lists.

30

Library for the Ages

Archaeologists have learned much about ancient Mesopotamia from discovering a library created by Assyria's last great ruler, Ashurbanipal (ah-shur-BAH-ni-pal). Ashurbanipal collected thousands of clay tablets containing information written by Sumerians, Babylonians, and Assyrians. These tablets contained poetry as well as information about medicine and science. One of the oldest poems ever written, a tale about the Sumerian king Gilgamesh (GIL-guh-mesh), was also found in the library.

Ashurbanipal's palace was built on the banks of the Tigris river.

A Sumerian cuneiform tablet

CHAPTER 5

Reading and Writing

Experts believe that, around 5,300 years ago, the Sumerians were the first people to use a writing system called **cuneiform** (kyoo-NEE-uh-form). Cuneiform was made up of different symbols that stood for objects and actions. The ancient Mesopotamians used cuneiform to write all of the different languages that they spoke.

Cuneiform writing was used for more than 2,500 years.

Written in Clay

The word *cuneiform* comes from Latin, and means "wedge-shaped." To write cuneiform, a tool known as a stylus was cut from a stalk of tall grass called a reed. As the stylus was pressed into a tablet of soft

A British soldier named Henry Rawlinson learned to translate cuneiform in the mid-1800s.

clay, it created a wedge-shaped mark. Different combinations of marks made signs. Each sign had a different meaning.

The Sumerians were the first to use cuneiform. Later, both the Assyrians and the Babylonians wrote cuneiform. As different groups of people used cuneiform over time, changes were made to different signs and writing became easier and faster. But not everyone could read or write cuneiform—it was the job of a group of people known as **scribes**. Scribes spent years learning cuneiform. When someone needed a contract written or a letter read, they would hire a scribe to do it.

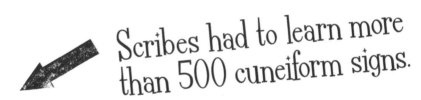

Scribes had to learn more than 500 cuneiform signs.

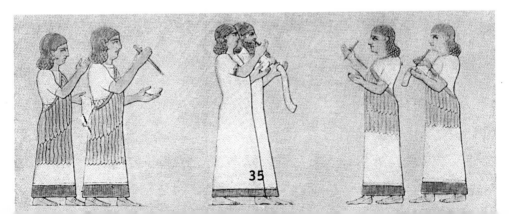

Keeping Records

At first, writing was mainly used to keep records. Government officials would write down how many sheep a family owned or how much barley they grew. But as time went on, people began to write down stories and poems, too. A poet named Enheduanna (en-HAY-doo-ann-uh) was the daughter of the Akkadian king Sargon. Enheduanna is the earliest known poet in the world.

This Babylonian map of the world dates from around 700 B.C.E.

Mesopotamian Math

Cuneiform writing included numbers as well as words. Much of the math we use today, like multiplication, was also used by the Mesopotamians thousands of years ago. The Babylonians are well known for their accomplishments in math including the study of shapes, or geometry. Understanding how to measure different shapes helped the Babylonians become master builders.

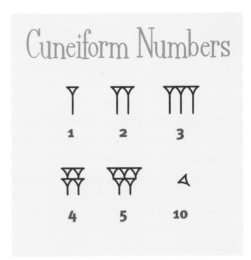

Cuneiform Numbers

1	2	3
4	5	10

The Ishtar Gate

The Babylonians were the first people to create buildings with arches and columns.

Today, some of the ruins of Babylon's walls have been rebuilt.

CHAPTER 6

The End of an Empire

During the time of Nebuchadnezzar II, New Babylonia was wealthy and very powerful. But after his death, the empire began to fall apart. The rulers who came after Nebuchadnezzar II were not very wise or strong. Eventually, their power over the empire weakened and New Babylonia was left open to attacks.

Nebuchadnezzar II built a wall around Babylon more than 11 miles (17 kilometers) long.

The Rise of Persia

While New Babylonia grew weaker, Persia, an empire to the east of Mesopotamia, became more and more powerful. In 539 B.C.E., the Persian emperor Cyrus the Great invaded and conquered Mesopotamia. He made his son, Cambyses (kam-BI-sees) II, king of Babylonia. The great age of Mesopotamian civilizations had come to an end.

The Persians ruled Mesopotamia for 200 years. In 331 B.C.E., they were conquered by the Greek army, led by Alexander the Great. The Greeks ruled for more than a hundred years. They were followed by the Arabs and the Turks.

Cyrus the Great and the Persian army entering Babylon

Gone but not Forgotten

Though the ancient Mesopotamian civilizations disappeared long ago, their contributions, such as cities, the wheel, and a writing system, continue to be an important part of our lives. Today, archaeologists are searching through ancient sites in Iraq and looking for clues from Mesopotamia. They hope to discover more about some of its ancient and important civilizations. ★

There are more than 10,000 archaeological sites in Iraq.

Length of the Tigris River: 1,180 mi. (1,900 km)

Length of the Euphrates River: 1,740 mi. (2,800 km)

Number of laws in Hammurabi's code: 282

Number of years cuneiform writing was used: More than 2,500

Number of works in Ashurbanipal's library: More than 20,000

Number of lions on the walls outside of the Ishtar Gate: About 120

Last known use of cuneiform: First century C.E.

Did you find the truth?

T The ancient Mesopotamians were the first to use the wheel.

F Persia was once part of ancient Mesopotamia.

Resources

Books

Foster, Karen Polinger. *The City of Rainbows: A Tale from Ancient Sumer*. Philadelphia: University of Pennsylvania Museum, 1999.

Hunt, Norman Bancroft. *Living in Ancient Mesopotamia*. New York: Chelsea House Publishers, 2009.

Hunter, Erica C.D. *Ancient Mesopotamia (Cultural Atlas for Young People)*. New York: Chelsea House Publishers, 2007.

Mehta-Jones, Shilpa. *Life in Ancient Mesopotamia*. New York: Crabtree Publishing, 2005.

Matthews, Rupert. *You Wouldn't Want to Be an Assyrian Soldier!: An Ancient Army You'd Rather Not Join*. Danbury, CT: Franklin Watts, 2007.

Oakes, Lorna. *Mesopotamia (Passport to the Past)*. New York: Rosen Publishing, 2009.

Shuter, Jane. *Mesopotamia*. Chicago: Heinemann Library, 2005.

Steele, Philip. *Mesopotamia*. New York: DK Publishing, 2007.

Organizations and Web Sites

The British Museum: Mesopotamia
www.mesopotamia.co.uk/menu.html
Explore an ancient Assyrian palace and much more in this site designed by the British Museum.

University of Pennsylvania Museum
www.museum.upenn.edu/new/exhibits/galleries/ mesopotamia.html
Write your name in cuneiform at this site!

Ancient Mesopotamia for Kids
www.mesopotamia.mrdonn.org
Read articles about Mesopotamian life and culture and find links to other cool sites.

Places to Visit

The Oriental Institute Museum
1155 East 58th Street
Chicago, IL 60637
(773) 702 9514
http://mesopotamia.lib. uchicago.edu/
View hundreds of artifacts on display in the museum's Mesopotamian Gallery.

The Metropolitan Museum of Art
1000 Fifth Avenue
at 82nd Street
New York, NY 10028-0198
(212) 535 7710
www.metmuseum.org
Stand in an Assyrian palace hall in the Sackler Gallery for Assyrian Art.

Important Words

archaeologists (ar-kee-OL-uh-jists) – scientists who study history by looking at artifacts

artifacts – objects that were made by people, such as tools or weapons

city-states – cities and the villages around them that have their own independent governments

civilizations (si-ve-li-ZAY-shens) – groups of people with a highly organized way of life

cuneiform (kyoo-NEE-uh-form) – an ancient writing system that used symbols made of wedge-shaped marks

empire – a group of countries or people under the control of one ruler or government

scribes – specially educated people in ancient times who were able to read and write

silt – a rich mud made from fine soil and particles from the bottom of a river or lake

ziggurats (ZIH-gur-ats) – tall platforms with many steps that usually had a temple at the top

Index

Page numbers in **bold** indicate illustrations.

About the Author

Sunita Apte still remembers learning about ancient Mesopotamia in the sixth grade at school. Her first taste of faraway lands and ancient cultures led to a lifelong interest in other places. When she's not writing children's books at home in Brooklyn, New York, Sunita travels the world with her family, often by bicycle.

PHOTOGRAPHS © 2010: Dave King, ©Dorling Kindersley, Courtesy of The Science Museum, London (wheel, p. 18); Getty Images (back cover; ziggurat, p. 5; p. 24; p. 26; pp. 28–29; p. 42); iStockphoto (©Cenk Ertekin, Euphrates River, p. 5; ©Fabio Bianchini, Uruk figure, p. 20); Photolibrary (pp. 9–10; pp. 14–15; p. 17; Ur chariot, p. 18; p. 19; ziggurat, p. 20; Assyrian figure, Ishtar Gate lion, p. 21; pp. 30–31; pp. 35–36; p. 38; p. 41; p. 43); Stockxpert (©Kate Duffell, p. 3); Tranz/Corbis (cover; p. 6; p. 16; Code of Hammurabi, p. 21; pp. 22–23; p. 27; p. 32; p. 34; p. 37)